IMPROVING YOUR RESILIENCE

How to bounce back after disappointment

Written by Nicolas Martin

Translated by Jessica Foster

Coaching 50MINUTES.com

50MINUTES.com
PROPEL
YOUR BUSINESS FORWARD!
NETWORKING
Venture outside your close circle
and connect with other professionals
Effective CV Writing
Resolving Office Conflict
Boost Your Concentration
Find Your Work-Life Balance
www.50minutes.com

RESILIENCE

- **Issue:** how do I develop or strengthen my resilience?
- **Uses:** although overcoming difficult moments sometimes seems impossible, every individual has, to different extents, the strength to continue making progress and to be happy. And since difficult moments in life are inevitable, it is better to learn how to use this strength and develop resilience, starting right now.
- **Professional context:** teamwork, personal management, stress management, etc.
- **FAQs:**
  - How is resilience different from coping or empowerment?
  - What are the main mechanisms in the resilience process?
  - How can I seek support from those around me without becoming unbearable?
  - Can everyone be resilient, or is resilience something you either have or you don't?
  - Can we completely heal after suffering?
  - Is a resilient person more likely to succeed professionally?

"What doesn't kill you makes you stronger", as the well-known saying goes. Currently, a very small circle of experts are working on the concepts of resilience and coping with suffering.

Every individual is supposed to have a natural predisposition as to their ability to deal with difficulties in their lives. This naturally manifests itself differently according to each person, as every instance of suffering is unique. Whether it is the loss of a loved one, an attack, a war, a natural disaster or a long period of unemployment, a break-up or a violent argument with a loved one, there is no hierarchy of suffering for the simple reason that every individual is different. Some people can find it very difficult to recover from a break-up, yet manage physical assault much more easily than others. The thing that everyone shares is the pain that results from it.

Living a life without difficult moments is a utopian vision, as suffering, whatever its cause, is simply inevitable. For this reason, it is essential to learn to deal with suffering and to get it under control and master it as much as possible. The cause of the pain is not particularly important, everyone must find in themselves the force to bounce back and keep going, as life continues on many levels, including professionally.

"As work plays a central role in our society, It is helpful to think in terms of it when considering this process of resilience and the ways in which it is possible to reinforce it, not because you have to keep working as if nothing happened, but because you owe it to yourself to keep making progress in the face of the good and the bad things that life has to offer you. Do not be resigned and within these thoughts and this advice you will find an approach that you will be able to adopt and that will help you to deal with difficult times with more flexibility. Some challenges seem difficult to overcome; others, which might however seem more traumatic to most people, can be managed more easily. And that is exactly what happened to me. I found it much more difficult to deal with criticism of a long, difficult piece of work than with physical assault.

"I was unlucky enough to be the victim of an assault when I was returning home one evening during the week. I say 'unlucky' because I have realised that I was simply in the wrong place at the wrong time. I had to go to hospital alone, it was already late and the police escorted me to Accident and Emergency. But during the days that followed, I was surrounded by people, in a way I could have never imagined. A flood of loved ones came to see me, and made me want to cry even more.

"I was not particularly traumatised after the event. I didn't really think about it, perhaps too occupied by the last few weeks of my final year of studying. I remember telling myself that it had to happen one day, and that it had now happened, and that it was therefore unlikely to happen again. This was something of a relief, and I told myself that I had reacted well at the time. I was almost pleased with myself, as the situation could have been much more serious and I could have ended up being much more traumatised.

"I think that I had started from a good basis at the beginning. I went through a stage of denial, but above all I turned the matter around in many ways, and humour played an important role.

"I believe that for every event that causes suffering, it is imperative to adopt a detached attitude, but this alone is not sufficient. Having the right people around you is necessary, as well as not allowing suffering to surpass laughter. Obviously, some instances of suffering leave little room for humour at the beginning, but above all, they should never become a taboo subject, as this is what substantially prevents any resilience process."

(Anonymous statement)

BEING A RESILIENT WORKER: THE BASICS

THE CONCEPT OF RESILIENCE AND GENERAL POINTS

Origin

The term 'resilience' was originally used in the context of physics, specifically material sciences such as metallurgy: it refers to a metal that can resist high impact and return to its original state after being beaten out of shape.

It is an interdisciplinary concept and has been borrowed by other disciplines, such as computer science, biology, mental health, humanities (such as psychology and sociology) and medicine. They have all kept the essence of the basic definition of the concept, namely the ability to restore original properties after an upset of some kind, while adapting it to the specifics of each discipline. Consequently, the term is sometimes used indiscriminately, and experts struggle to agree on one definition that can satisfy everyone.

In Europe, the concept was first used in psychology in the 1990s, mainly by psychiatrists or child psychiatrists. One of the most prominent voices on the subject is Boris Cyrulnik, a French psychiatrist, whose work *Un merveilleux malheur* ('Miraculous Unhappiness'), published in 1999, was the first to contribute to the exposure of resilience.

Although it has been studied within the scientific community for several decades, the concept itself is therefore relatively recent, while its application in psychology only became truly popular in the 2000s.

Definition

Generally speaking, the word 'resilience' has been adopted in different domains to refer to the ability to bounce back or tolerate shocks without being destroyed. Its psychological definition is based on the definition suggested by Manciaux, Vanistendael, Lecomte and Cyrulnik in 2001, which refers to the ability of a person or group to continue making progress and planning for the future despite traumatising events or difficult living conditions.

In other words, resilience refers to the personal quality that every individual possesses and that allows them to overcome a difficult or traumatic event, and to continue to build their lives and find fulfilment in the face of adversity.

RESILIENCE, A PROCESS

We need to picture resilience as a process. Indeed, even if it initially refers to a state and can be seen as a character trait or a result of other factors in several contexts, when applied to individuals, we are generally talking about progressive, non-definitive change. An individual's capacity for resilience is constantly reassessed, as everyone changes throughout their lives, just as each of life's challenges is different; all these changes are part of a process.

A particularly current concept

The success that the notion of resilience has experienced can partly be explained by the message of hope it brings. Indeed, according to this theory, nobody is condemned to being unhappy, even those whose lives start out in the worst conditions. It is always possible to get out of that state, nothing is forever. The concept of destiny is questioned and, in this way, resilience offers a positive dynamic and fills us with hope.

This term is echoed particularly these days by the tendency towards individualism in our societies. Now, it is the individual who matters most of all, which drives them to be more demanding about their own personal fulfilment. All of life's difficulties can consequently become a real test. That obviously does not mean that we currently suffer more than we did in the past, but rather that we suffer differently and, above all, that everyone has become more attentive to their feelings and their development in the face of life's challenges. In a way, everyone has become more vulnerable as they are more exposed to their feelings.

Additionally, in an extremely volatile economic, political and social context, it is even more likely that a person will have not just one, but several difficult periods in their life. However, the examples constantly demonstrate that despite the difficulty of the challenges faced, a person can pick themselves up again due to their willpower, their inner strength and their capacity for resilience – which is where the need to understand how this process works and how to gain greater resistance in the face of life's casualties comes from.

UNDERSTANDING THE MECHANISMS AND PROCESSES

Resilience factors

Many studies have been carried out on different groups of people who have lived through difficult and traumatic situations (war, poverty, illness, etc.). These studies have helped us to discern different categories of resources that promote resilience, which might concern individuals, families, communities or societies. We can thus generally differentiate between four main levels of resilience, under which the different factors are classified:

- individual resilience (resources in your personality)
- family resilience (resources from family relationships)
- community resilience (resources from the community)
- social or societal resilience (resources found in society).

N.B.

Some approaches group community resilience and social or societal resilience on the same level, and therefore classify the factors into three main categories instead of four.

Here is a more detailed look at some of the factors that facilitate resilience, to give you an idea of the different elements present around you.

Resilience factors

Individual resilience factors	• Intelligence • Skills • Easy-going temperament • Flexibility • Sense of humour • Self-esteem • Maturity • Academic qualifications • Introspection • Gender and age • Feeling of usefulness • Ability to anticipate the future • Good sense of identity • Spiritual orientation	• Internal control • Problem-solving habits • Independence • Ability to distance themselves from an upsetting environment • Social skills • Empathy • Altruism • Sociability and popularity • Perception of a positive relationship with an adult
Family resistance factors	• Parents' age • Number of children (under 5) • Gap between births • Adequate physical space • Support and affection • Spirituality and ideology • Educational discipline • Fairness within the family • Opportunities for participation • Quality of communication • Warm and positive interactions	• Child seen as a resource, with a future • Ability to face the unexpected • Conflict resolution abilities • Sharing values • Stable financial situation • Non-possessiveness • Lack of separation at a young age • Presence of a paternal figure

Community resilience factors	• Peers • Social community: school, neighbourhood, associations, etc. • Religious or ideological community • Solidarity • Raised expectations • Opportunities to get involved	• Values of mutual aid and social tolerance • Diversity of support and social resources • Good levels of healthcare, training, accommodation, care, leisure activities and transport
Social or societal resilience factors	• Values of mutual aid and social tolerance • Raised expectations • Opportunities • Social and political laws to fight poverty • Strict laws on gun control • Supported anti-violence messages in the media and elsewhere • Society and culture • Low levels of unemployment • Low levels of crime	

PRACTICAL ADVICE

It is therefore possible, in our own way and on a regular basis, to take stock of these factors in order to be aware of the ones we possess and that can aid the resilience process.

We will mostly analyse the first category of factors here, as it is the one on which any individual can act, particularly in a professional setting. Additionally, it is possible to simplify the classification and to reduce the factors that allow us to evaluate our capacity for resilience to seven. These are all linked to personality, but the family and community environment can play an important role in their development:

- perceptiveness
- independence
- interpersonal skills
- initiative
- creativity
- humour
- morality.

The better equipped a person is with these characteristics, the more likely they are to quickly recover after an upset; these factors can therefore be used as indicators of resilience. We must be careful, however, as some variables can seriously slow down the resilience process despite everything, such as the intensity of the trauma, the suddenness of the attack, our mental health prior to the upset or a lack of social, professional and cultural relationships.

Resilience mechanisms

Resilience, part of the movement known as 'positive psychology', is a dynamic process which allows a person or a group who have undergone a trauma to pick themselves up again and lead a life which they find satisfying. It is helpful to add the 'evolving' character of this dynamic process, as it goes without saying that resilience is never acquired once and for all. And while most experts on the subject explain that it is acquired during childhood, the fact remains that it is a fundamental ability that each individual has and that we can develop. Everyone is capable of transforming their reality, provided that they can draw, from themselves and their surroundings, everything they need to start the process and generate this capacity for resilience.

Boris Cyrulnik identifies eight mechanisms that allow us to recover after an upset:

- self-protection;
- balance when faced with tensions;
- 'challenge-commitment', refusing to let yourself be beaten, defying suffering;
- rebounding, no longer putting up with suffering, but becoming the active subject of your own life once more;
- evaluation, or coming to terms with the trauma;
- meaning evaluation, or the meaning given to the challenge;
- positivity;
- creativity, changing perspective, constructing something new and stronger.

Each of these eight mechanisms leads to greater resilience. A person will tend to take one path instead of another based on their personal experience and their innate preferences. In this way, someone who has, for example, been abandoned by one of their parents will undoubtedly show some predispositions to use the logic of self-protection. A positive person who has been through a great emotional ordeal might decide to implement their positivity mechanisms to overcome this disappointment, or even undertake a process of 'challenge-commitment' by trying again.

On a professional level, there is no mechanism that works better than another. But it is important to be aware of them, as coming to terms with issues is often very beneficial and allows us to continue to strengthen our capacity for resilience. Moreover, it is possible to try several options, at the same time or successively, to overcome an obstacle.

DEVELOPING OUR RESILIENCE

It is essential to understand the factors, mechanisms and processes that allow us to develop our resilience in case of a particularly difficult event. But this is just one step that allows us to lay the groundwork.

Stefan Vanistendael (born 1951), sociologist, demographer and deputy chief administrative officer, in charge of research and development at BICE (International Catholic Child Bureau), has highlighted that two elements are essential for creating the basis for resilience: connections and mea-ningfulness. Taking these as a starting point, here are some concrete methods you can try to explore in order to improve your resilience.

Establish social connections

The relationships you have with those around you, your family and friends, are very important. The support you re-ceive from your loved ones can be a determining factor. But look at the bigger picture too. Some professional contacts, some acquaintances or some people you know but with whom contact is less regular can also offer you support that you would not necessarily have expected. Spend time with these people too as soon as the opportunity presents itself. You will have to trust your instincts to distinguish who will be able to support you when you are going through a difficult period.

Regularly take time for yourself

Seeking support from those around you does not mean solely and exclusively relying on other people. When we are going through difficult times, it is essential to listen to ourselves and our most basic wishes, such as buying ourselves something nice to eat, having an evening in watching a series, exercising, going to a particular place with a book or to listen to music, etc. Everyone is sensitive to certain little things that lift our spirits. Identify what you enjoy and what revitalises you. While relaxation exercises have undeniable benefits, everyone relaxes in their own way.

Try introspection and a deeper analysis of the situation

Even if this might seem unappealing, it is often necessary to think through all the aspects of a difficult situation, whether on a personal or an external level. Many people are already aware of certain elements, and this first realisation is already a great step forward, as it means that work has started to be done. It is however still essential to see this introspection process through to the end, in order to be able to then make the decisions required with full knowledge of the facts.

Rely on optimism and a positive attitude

This might seem clichéd, but thinking optimistically and positively is something that can be worked on in the long term, in order to make it into a true lifestyle choice. People who tend to live in fear and who are constantly on edge end up causing the very events that they wanted to avoid and think of them as inevitable. Developing optimism and a positive attitude can be done on a day-to-day basis, as much in small everyday details as in more important matters. In any case, try to be aware of what you are thinking and to review it if it is a pessimistic vision – leading to discouragement, self-denigration and inaction – with the aim of changing it into something more positive.

Make humour a way of life

Of course, not everyone is programmed the same when it comes to humour; however, everyone likes to laugh and smile. When we are capable of laughing in a serious or difficult situation, the process of detachment from it is already well on its way. This cannot be done in a day, but whatever happens, do not let a difficult period of your life take away your ability to laugh and make jokes. Humour is a powerful tool and an extremely strong factor of resilience, and it allows you to see things in a new light and to be more relaxed about them. Take care, however, not to use it solely as a barrier to grief and refuse to explore the problem in more depth.

Keep an eye on your diet

Studies have shown that there is a very strong link between what you eat, your physical condition and your stress levels. Surviving a traumatic event or getting through a difficult situation is demanding on our physical strength. When we are tired, we tend to forget about exercise or healthy eating, and the vicious cycle continues. Pay attention to these physical warning signs; eat healthily, exercise and above all, pay attention to your sleep patterns, as their benefits are extremely well-known.

See a healthcare professional

Some people need additional support and health professionals are certainly effective. While demonstrating resilience is an extremely useful quality, some situations can exacerbate symptoms of depression or anxiety. While some individuals still feel able to draw on their own resources to deal with these events, others will not think twice before seeking a specialist. More and more people are regularly making the most of this kind of support.

GAINING STRENGTH ON A PROFESSIONAL LEVEL

Many organisations have understood the need to develop resilience as much at the managerial level as at the employee level. Since everyone is likely to be faced at some point with particularly long working hours, a significant workload or a stressful environment, It Is completely logical that research is gradually progressing on the subject, and organisations are accepting it and implementing training or tools to help this process along and avoid any difficult situations at work or resulting from work.

Why is resilience so important from an organisational or professional point of view? Essentially because understanding what allows us to develop resilience is becoming increasingly urgent in a global context of high competition, complexity, crises and constant change. Implementing mechanisms that enable workers to develop resilience is therefore fundamental in that, on the one hand, an organisation's ability to adapt mostly depends on its employees' ability to adapt, but on the other hand, the constantly changing global context limits every individual in their ability to anticipate and adapt to these organisational changes. This is a paradoxical situation which can therefore potentially be a source of difficulties on a professional level.

On an individual level

Gilles Teneau, a French expert on resilience within organisations, has studied several aspects of this, notably the positive effects of resilient people on organisations, which limits the stress of their co-workers. Known as "toxic handlers", these individuals are capable of spreading energy, actively listening and calming tense relationships, while staying out of games of power that are traditionally at play in the world of work. We can identify them through several characteristics:

- their ability to empathise with others' emotions;
- their ability to give meaning to events;

- their ability to unconditionally accept others.

Knowing how to identify these people allows us to draw inspiration from them. These individuals, whether they have developed a certain level of resilience after an upsetting event or whether they have managed to build up this resilience over the years, allow a team – and, by extension, a company – to work within very contemporary logic, completely different from the classic reasoning on professional organisation.

On an organisational level

For their part, organisations also have a role to play. They can work on different aspects to build their employees' resilience without waiting to run into a problem, as resilient individuals are high-performing individuals. Jean-Christophe Barralis, a French psychotherapist, has also worked on these questions, starting from the premise that exchanges on the strengths and successes of a team lead to creativity, hope, motivation and commitment.

Practically speaking, the development of resilience can be initiated and supported by the organisation and therefore by the board of directors and/or the managerial team through specific actions:

- identifying the strengths and assets of employees and relying on these observations in order to manage them;
- focusing attention on successes;
- making work as meaningful as possible;
- understanding the employees' working conditions

(workload);
- cultivating an atmosphere of trust;
- encouraging cohesion, cooperation, mutual assistance and generosity;
- encouraging independence;
- facilitating the spread of positive emotions;
- recognising effort as much as results;
- setting an example.

OBSTACLES AND RISKS

Resilience is a useful concept for those who want to continue to make progress despite the upsets that life has in store for us. But developing your resilience is not always simple and the path towards a healthy, balanced lifestyle is full of obstacles. Knowing how to identify them, anticipate them and be fully aware of them allows us, on the one hand, not to endanger the work we have done, and on the other hand to start again from new bases that are even more stable, as resilience relies on understanding all the mechanisms at work. So which obstacles can interfere?

- Some people are unable to come to terms with their suffering, insofar as the reality is too difficult to accept and the trauma is too significant. They do not have a clear vision of the factors that are at play, are unable to understand where their suffering is coming from, what it causes them to feel, etc. We are not, however, talking about denial, as the person will have a confused understanding that there is a problem and will attempt to come to terms with it, without actually getting past this stage. If we follow Boris Cyrulnik's logic, when this process is not possible or is made difficult, the individual is unable to gain control over their trauma and their capacity for resilience is greatly compromised.
- Another risk lies in the attachment that is sometimes developed towards suffering. This should not be ignored. Some people are aware of having experienced a traumatic event but, instead of beginning a rebuilding process, will end up in a dangerous relationship with the suffering they have endured. Some people are also happy to wallow in their suffering, choosing the ease of playing the victim rather than putting in the effort to fight to bounce back again.
- Additionally, showing resilience does not mean acting tough, being completely unshakeable or taking everything upon yourself without asking for help from anyone, as solitude is the surest way of preventing resilience.

While it is of course sometimes good to refocus on yourself to deal with some difficult situations, cutting yourself off from everything and everyone risks overly weakening the resilient foundations that we thought we had built.

- On the other hand, some individuals tend to rely completely on other people and ignore the personal and individual aspects of the process. While it is sometimes difficult to find a balance between these two aspects, it is however possible to become aware of it, notably when you do not feel capable of being alone even for one day. The people around you are of course an essential source of support, but developing your resilience by yourself and for yourself is also necessary.
- On the way, some people will be tempted to use the logic of denial, thinking that it is a solid basis. But denying that your suffering exists works against the mechanisms that allow you to develop true capacities for resilience.

In all cases, flexibility will be your closest ally. Developing your resilience involves arming your capacity for resilience against various kinds of upset. We do not become resilient once and for all; we reuse these abilities under different forms that are adapted to the situation at hand. Thus, faced with a colleague criticising your presentation, you might think about using humour; dealing with the death of a friend, you will seek comfort from loved ones who will be able to offer you support, etc.

As resilience is neither definitive nor fixed, it is therefore a balance that is reached between managing the negative aspects of suffering or trauma and our capacity to derive strength from them, allowing us to continue to live in a healthy and calm way. But this balance is fragile, for the simple reason that difficult situations happen and they rarely resemble one another. It is therefore necessary to try to adapt and constantly change your resilience mechanisms, even when we believe we have become strong enough to resist anything. It is a continuous process, a lifestyle, and a way of thinking and acting that allows us to become gradually more capable of dealing with difficult situations by drawing on our capacity to think differently.

TOP TIPS

- Maintain and prioritise social contact. Your social network – family, friends and acquaintances – plays and will always play an essential role. All these people will allow you to find help and support during difficult times. Consequently, extending this network means increasing your chances of finding comfort when you need it, while paying attention and listening to other people can only have beneficial effects. So why not get involved in an association or an organisation, for example?
- Do not tell yourself that periods of crisis are insurmountable. You cannot prevent certain things from being particularly difficult and stressful to go through. On the other hand, you can change your way of interpreting these difficult times to face up to them in a less resigned way. Be positive! You need to try and look past the situation and imagine yourself in more pleasant circumstances. There is absolutely no reason that you will be deprived of happy moments forever.
- Accept that change is part of life. Everything changes, including you. The important thing is to be able to go along with these changes and adapt.
- Set yourself objectives. That does not mean being inflexible or wanting to reach these objectives at literally any cost. You have to make progress in this direction, by accomplishing things that bring you closer to it every day. You will gradually get into a virtuous dynamic and you will develop with much more determination and flexibility.

- Be firm in your decisions. You can always take action against the setbacks by demonstrating firmness in your choices and decisions. Act on the things on which you can have an influence.
- Look for opportunities to explore your personality. A difficult situation is also a way of seeing yourself in a new light and becoming more resilient. Experiencing periods of crisis and managing to overcome them allows you to better manage your social relationships, have better self-esteem, feel stronger even if you are still sometimes vulnerable, better appreciate the different things that make up life and make the most of them.
- Keep a positive image of yourself. Develop confidence in your ability to resolve problems. Over the years, everyone starts to get to know themselves and know how they work. Try to identify the methods you have implemented that have already helped you to feel better in bad situations; you will be able to react to them appropriately and more easily.
- Keep things in perspective. We tend to blow some things out of proportion at times. Instead, try to frame the elements in a broader context, understand what might have led to this situation or why you are reacting in this way. Understanding is a key component.
- Trust in the future and what it has to offer you, as optimism leads to fortunate events. Moreover, it is always more constructive to try to visualise what you are aspiring to than to fear whatever might prevent you from reaching it.
- Accept who you are, your past and your circumstances. Accept the way in which certain things have happened

and the way in which others will happen, but also accept that you have the possibility to influence and change certain situations. It is sometimes useful to tell yourself that something is not right, that you are going through a rough time, that you are losing morale and that this is a fact. Using that as a starting point, think about what you already have in your life that might allow you to get yourself back on track and show resilience. Try to identify what might work for you and your situation. You will then be able to reproduce this pattern after adapting it slightly.

FAQS

HOW IS RESILIENCE DIFFERENT FROM COPING OR EMPOWERMENT?

Even if the precise limits of the definition of the concept of resilience are up for discussion, resilience brings an additional nuance to the concepts of coping or empowerment.

- **Coping** aims to strengthen the individual's ability to manage anxiety and control their fears. It is the collection of efforts and processes used by an individual between themselves and an event that is perceived as threatening or stressful, to control, tolerate or minimise the impact of the event on their physical and psychological wellbeing. It is also about learning to face up to adversity through any means possible.
- **Empowerment** is a process or approach that aims to allow individuals to have greater powers of action and decision, as well as more influence on their environment and their lives. It supposes that every individual has potential and resources and must be able to use them to improve their living conditions and to move towards fairness.
- **Resilience**, however, has an extra nuance compared with these two concepts, in that it allows us to overcome the negative and progress in a positive way to continue to live as well as possible. Coping and empowerment do not necessarily include this aspect of overall wellbeing. It is only a question of responding to difficult situations using different methods, without worrying about whether the

result will be profoundly positive on a psychological or physical level.

WHAT ARE THE MAIN MECHANISMS IN THE RESILIENCE PROCESS?

Specialists on the subject have found several mechanisms which individuals who have been through a particularly difficult event implement, sometimes successively, to counter this negative trajectory:

- self-protection
- balance when faced with tensions
- 'challenge-commitment'
- rebounding
- evaluation
- meaning evaluation
- positivity
- creativity.

Within these mechanisms, we can identify some tools that allow them to be applied, such as humour, a resilience factor that is particularly well-developed in people who are resistant to life's difficulties. This ability to use a form of self-deprecation in the face of trauma highlights a true acceptance and a desire to not wallow in sadness as well as to stop being perceived as a victim by others.

Some people choose denial, thinking that seeming strong will protect them from the pity of those around them and will prevent the effects of the traumatising event. Denial is, however, not strictly speaking a resilience mechanism, as this pure and simple rejection is based on ignoring the traumatic event rather than understanding or accepting it in order to change it. Denial leads to internal fragility that endangers the process in its entirety.

HOW CAN I SEEK SUPPORT FROM THOSE AROUND ME WITHOUT BECOMING UNBEARABLE?

The people around you – family, friends and acquaintances – play an essential role. They allow you to talk about your suffering and to see it in a new light to learn how to have more control over it. But it is also important to be able to put these people at ease about the topic when you talk about it. They must not feel like it is a taboo subject and that they have to walk on eggshells to talk about it freely and constructively. It is therefore by having previously managed to play down the suffering in your mind that you will really be able to seek support from those around you.

CAN EVERYONE BE RESILIENT OR IS RESILIENCE SOMETHING YOU EITHER HAVE OR YOU DON'T?

Starting from the principle that everyone has, within themselves, abilities that allow them to overcome suffering and continue to make progress towards all other kinds of happiness, in theory everyone can demonstrate resilience. On the other hand, resilience is never fully acquired; it is a continuous process that everyone works on throughout their lives.

One thing is certain: there is a dichotomy that exists when confronted with suffering. We can either let ourselves be beaten or fight against it. This choice depends on the people and the situations: some people will decide to fully implement resilience mechanisms so that they do not remain victims of this suffering; others will not be aware of the abilities they have and will choose other alternatives, such as denial, at the risk of dragging their suffering around with them under different forms.

CAN WE COMPLETELY HEAL AFTER SUFFERING?

Resilience is not a miracle solution that allows us to live without ever thinking about the suffering we have endured as if it never happened. We need to understand that the objective is to succeed and to piece ourselves back together after the difficulties we have faced. Suffering is thus often controlled and transformed, but is never lost entirely. Nonetheless, this suffering no longer slows down personal development or a happy life, as it has been transformed into a life force.

IS A RESILIENT PERSON MORE LIKELY TO SUCCEED PROFESSIONALLY?

Professional success does not depend on a person's capacity for resilience. On the other hand, demonstrating resilience at work allows the creation of a virtuous circle which can potentially lead to good management of problems, a better perception of the opportunities that present themselves, or becoming a pillar of the team.

Resilient people tend to give off healthy and positive energy. They will be more capable of dealing with small, regular sources of pressure and longer periods of stress, without offloading them onto other people or keeping them to themselves. Additionally, these people will be more likely to be the source of new ideas and new ways of perceiving the situations that arise: they will often suggest more innovative ways of doing things that are better adapted to the problems faced.

Demonstrating resilience allows us, above all, to adopt a positive logic by trusting the future, which allows us to bear potential professional upsets with more flexibility and to not let ourselves be destabilised by unexpected events.

OVER TO YOU

Stefan Vanistendael and Jacques Lecomte, in their 2000 work *Le bonheur est toujours possible* ('Happiness is Always Possible'), summarised the components of resilience in the form of a small house called the *casita*. This model offers a visual summary of all the elements of the start of the resilience process and their importance; it can allow you to lay the foundations so that you understand more what you already have and what you are lacking or what is not yet stable enough to guarantee effective development.

While the *casita* must certainly be adapted depending on your personal situation, the two authors insist on the fact that it is a powerful symbol as the house and the household usually give a feeling of security and support. The connections between rooms, which communicate or don't, allow us to clearly visualise the different elements and points of interest: resilience is constructed based on several factors which interact with each other. It is up to you to decide what these factors are for you.

The casita

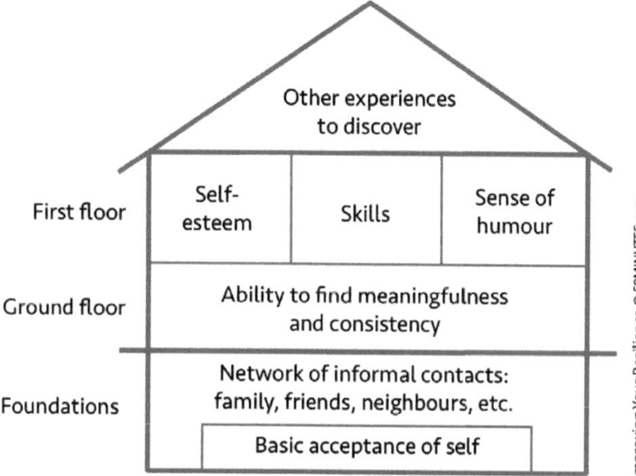

Other experiences
to discover
First floor
Self-esteem
Skills
Sense of humour
Ground floor
Ability to find meaningfulness
and consistency
Foundations
Network of informal contacts:
family, friends, neighbours, etc.
Basic acceptance of self
Improving Your Resilience © 50MINUTES.com

We want to hear from you!
Leave a comment on your online library
and share your favourite books on social media!

FURTHER READING

BIBLIOGRAPHY

- Anaut, M. (2005) Le concept de résilience et ses applications cliniques. *Cairn.info.* [Online]. [Accessed 16 June 2015]. Available from: <http://www.cairn.info/zen.php?ID_ARTICLE=RSI_082_0004>
- Brissiaud, P. Y. (2001) *Surmonter ses blessures. De la maltraitance à la résilience.* Thonex: Jouvence.
- Brissiaud, P. Y. (2008) *La face cachée de la résilience. Guérir vraiment ses blessures intérieures.* Thonex: Jouvence.
- Cyrulnik, B. (1993) *Les nourritures affectives.* Paris: Odile Jacob.
- Cyrulnik, B. (2002) *Un merveilleux malheur.* Paris: Odile Jacob.
- Cyrulnik, B. (2009) *La résilience ou comment renaître de sa souffrance ?.* Paris: Odile Jacob.
- Cyrulnik, B. (2012) *Résilience. Connaissances de base.* Paris: Odile Jacob.
- Péters, S. (2013) La résilience au travail... C'est possible !. *LaTribune.fr.* [Online]. [Accessed 16 June 2015]. Available from: <http://www.latribune.fr/blogs/mieux-dans-mon-job/20131127trib000798064/la-resilience-au-travail-c-est-possible-.html>
- Péters, S. (2014) La résilience au travail. *LeMonde.fr.* [Online]. [Accessed 16 June 2015]. Available from: <http://www.lemonde.fr/emploi/article/2014/08/05/la-resilienceau-travail_4439006_1698637.html>
- Vanistendael, S. and Lecomte, J. (2000) *Le bonheur est*

toujours possible. Construire la résilience. Paris: Bayard.

IMPROVE YOUR GENERAL KNOWLEDGE

IN A BLINK OF AN EYE !

www.50minutes.com